T0077482

Allegories of the Everyday

Allegories of the Everyday

Dryad Press (Pty) Ltd
Postnet Suite 281, Private Bag X16 Constantia, 7848,
Cape Town, South Africa
www.dryadpress.co.za
business@dryadpress.co.za

Cover design and typography: Stephen Symons
Editor: Michèle Betty
Copy Editor: Helena Janisch

Set in 9.5/14pt Palatino Linotype
Printed and bound by Digital Action (Pty) Ltd

First published in Cape Town by Dryad Press (Pty) Ltd, 2019

ISBN 978-0-6398091-2-0

Allegories of the Everyday

Poems by

Brian Walter

Still at work, time shifts the stanzas,
scratches a line, evokes – for unity –
an old theme again, always moving chunks
of life away from childhood, and into age.

– Brian Walter

CONTENTS

I

II

I

He told us that both white and black deads were living in the Deads' Town, not a single alive was there at all. Because everything that they were doing there was incorrect to alives and everything that all alives were doing was incorrect to deads too.

– Amos Tutuola, The Palm-Wine Drinkard

Ordinary Water

I did not satisfy with it as palm-wine.
– Amos Tutuola, *The Palm-Wine Drinkard*

This has been a year of wakes
with three friends gone,
each a fellow on this dark
and sorry way through woods
to the simple place of the dead,
with whom I so easily drank,
embraced in the night inns,
whom I travelled with by day.

So I've drunk tributes to each,
falling – a drunken poet –
down the bar-house stair;
and I was bitten by a dog
that I, so pissed, petted
despite my host's appeals,
putting my guitar finger
out of joint; or sloshed,
rubbed with lost fingertips
the shoulder of the widow,
kindly kneading keening flesh
to keep a friend conjured there:

drunk – till I am done, and return
to the strange light of this world
where citizens toil, maybe screw
each other for a buck, or shoot

or stab at human flesh, or develop
someone's land for cash –
in this poor world where I must
drink, again, ordinary water.

Quest

Bird Island, Lambert's Bay

When the trusty wine tapster
of the palm-wine drinkard dies,
it's the old loss of a workless
paradise, or of his own psyche,
or that mid-way failing of soul;

and then the old wise folk tell
that all those recently gone
always dwell a while in a place
somewhere in this world.
So he sets out himself to find
the occupation of the dead –

the artist daily lifts old eyes
to the sea, and walks the sands
of a million million flecks of shell
to ponder the psyche, and mulls
the allegories of death with us,
underfoot, and over the land,

and witnesses the shores awash
with the old passing tides,
to find that life is urgent still –

as time nests here, and spawns,
and swims with the twisting seals,
flying with the gannets and gulls.

Really

… the gentleman left the really road
on which we were travelling and branched
into an endless forest…
– Amos Tutuola, *The Palm-Wine Drinkard*

Eyes only, and woods, and eternity
stalk this side of imagination,
where we walk with riding basket
and evensong, and words

packed like parcels. Stop. Wait
and listen, where the woods creak
and moan with unmoving silence.

Reach out for a human hand –
we'll find one day
what we always seek, and go

that really road back home.

Nilotic Triad

i. Taken

The dead have broken pieces
of myself,

cracked my mind
and memory

and drawn my blood
to take with them;

have carried wine and bread
away, across the waters

to the west bank of the Nile,
the dead land

where daily
the sun still

sets.

ii. Dead

We'd pass poems on,
or read them to each other,

till you became a third ear.
An eye. Then you died.

I write into empty time.
The waters of the Nile run north.

Sweet memory
flow softly

till I end
my song.

iii. De-colonising

Old Greenwich took
with science the right
to divide us up in hours,
overruling the mystery
of the old meridians:

but should the ley line
of dividing time
be smack down the Nile,

we'd know with better
certainty where
in this world

we stood.

Deads' Town Path

I'm alone with my head
these days:
all my friends are dead

and I walk the drought,
body and psyche
inside out,

those who knew me,
gone. The paths eroded
in my mind,

the well-trodden roads
of over-and-over
lament,

and old, and leaf-shaken,
I try to find a thought
not taken.

The Trek

Beneath all craic and comedy,
the palm-wine drinkard
on his solemn quest is a god, and yet
still filled with human fear and blood

as both you and I might be, and filled
with all our glee and playful curiosity –

his Faithful-Mother in her White Tree,
the rooted woman firm on our earth,
reaches out as he flees from the snare
of Unreturnable-Heaven, the God-foe.

And he and his wife betray each other,
cheat themselves at the old tree,
as is fitting, and there they sell
their deaths, but not their human fear;

and in the large hall of virtue's dance
the Faithful-Mother makes miracle wine…

We recognise the elements, can know
the spiritual trek, the happy allegory,
and can plumb the grave and comic ways
our deep, and old, and endless pathways go.

After Deads' Town

At Deads' Town he finds that the deads
walk, of course, only backwards
while he still treads like us, with his face;
and that the deads don't like our blood.

And so, with his new eyes, he proves
the sheer difference there, and grasps
the strong immediacy of the laws,
knowing quickly that he cannot stay –

though the dead and long-lost tapster must;
so he swigs, for last times, the good palm-wine
from his homely tapster – for three days
living in the shades of the lifeless zone.

At last, walking home to his living town,
the young deads, along the road, scorn him
and he's chased back to the roadless bush,
our naked world, our unbuilt labyrinth.

But, from the dead, he's borne the world's egg
and becomes such a judge that he can steady
earth and sky, setting the world in its place
below in balance. But our man-judge-god

won't crack the unsolvable mysteries
but passes them to us, living readers,
passes on his old quest to visit death
and grapple with our unknowing, as all

good story tellers do, or fine drinkards,
on this laughing, trying and troubled earth.

Guadeloupe

Past thirty now I know
To love the self is dread
Of being swallowed by the blue
Of heaven overhead
Or rougher blue below.
– Derek Walcott, 'Crusoe's Island'

i. Turning

The Atlantic is deep blue –
from this plane it looks like sky,
and the clouds down there like clouds
up against the firmament,

turning my mind upside down.
To get it right I need to peer
down hard, and find that rough
solidity of the wave ripples,

and I search in vain for a ship
to give my mind its bearings,
to punctuate the endless blue
with a dash of sense, to help me find
where I am, which way, and who.

ii. *Trompe l'œil*

Somewhere
the sky merges with ocean

and blue and blue become
one deep wash of aerial-marine

– old elements harmonise
and one canvas spans

from dome
to depth.

So, when the plane banks,
that ocean liner

– going our way
off the starboard side –

flies,

fellow travelling
in our watery skies.

iii. Disembarked

This looks so like Nigeria,
he says. And it does, and does not:
for the island topples our thoughts
in a topsy-turvy land that is,

and is not, with ways both new
and old in this Caribbean town.
Deads' Town echoes our ways –
so that questing drinkard found;

and on an isle of sugar cane and slaves,
her forts as round as Martello towers,
this poor plot in the tropics of spice
where trios of brown pelicans plunge,

where the tempest *Maria* flattened
forests, rooted up rich banana farms
and sloshed such water from the skies
that struck chaos in the elements –

on this slip of Africa cut and planted,
made French, the old motherland bent
insular, men made seafarers or fishers,
our grasp of things spins upside down.

Lapwent

i.

I roam the streets of Point-à-Pitre
and mark the residential flats,
the buildings both unkempt and spruce,
and consider that to maintain a home
on this isle of the tropics must be hell,
fretting in daily deep humidity
and toiling in the rough face of tempests
when the palm-bowing hurricanoes spout,
where wild *Maria*'s wrecks are twisted, still.

I mark the huge church, the schools
at work with children's shouts,
corner shops, and kitchen vans kitted out,
driven by generators, where folk sell.
Here a man trades at a simple table
his single dish, sitting like Patience;

while – outside a deathly silent door –
there sprawls an emblematic guy
long lounging in his plastic chair,
his hat drawn darkly over his face,
while old time runs down his legs
and back to earth: let the world blow away,
it seems he wouldn't know, or care.

And so, I walk amongst the living, here,
setting myself quite pointedly adrift
to wander amongst the quick mundane
so that our simple allegories can show.

ii.

There's a beckoning place, quiet and quaint,
up a side street, where I want to be:
a white-painted village, with such old-world
tumbled-up small houses, a dinky town,

a veranda here, or soft glass windows,
magical, and I'm drawn by quietness,
by the orderly retreat. Up ahead
I see crosses, like it's a holy space:

but not a foot stirs. There's an open gate,
so I walk in – and then, I know the place:
sepulchres, mausoleums, and old tombs
of generations – the Town of the Dead!

iii.

Those small residences for the lifeless,
hundreds with their little *stoeps*, leading steps,
roadways and paths, all beckon with family
names, candles and flowers – and yesterday

was All Souls Day, and all the living came.
Now, behind glass, cold candles wait.
Pictures of the dead watch me, intruder
with fleshy weight, out of time, oozing fate.

iv.

My mind is quick to shift and trip
all along the verandas, the *stoeps*,
and flits up the quaint steps, behind
the glass, finding squat candles spent.

Open eyes wander, up and down
beguiling roadways and brown dips,
up the hill and far over the dead town
of crosses and of family names.

One man washes his sins and body
before his people, another youth skulks
down the way of the many deaths,
retreating from my face.

Eyes upon me, all history
watches. The eyes behind the glass
see right through – deconstruct – me
till I become but figurative myself,

alone, with a pale face, walking dead
roads amongst the slave-fields
of sugar cane and forts: where my living flesh
– whatever I do or say or become –
is but someone else's allegory.

II

Now, at the rising of Venus – the steady star
that survives translation, if one can call this lamp
the planet that pierces us over indigo islands –
despite the critical sand flies, I accept my function
as a colonial upstart at the end of an empire,
a single, circling, homeless satellite.

– Derek Walcott, 'North and South'

Home Countree

I try to clear my desk
and mind

– what can fill the blankness
of death, and death, and more death –

I clear away the notes,
paid bills and lists ticked off,

phone numbers I can no longer place.
But my space for words is void.

A squall moved through yesterday
with a little welcome rain.

I try to put that down, write images
and feeling out of this deep futility.

But the soil here is sandy
and water slips off as from oil.

Nothing soaks in.
Nothing grows in the sterility.

In the sand under the eaves,
no rain wakes the dust,

not a syllable drops.

Muse

I forget things more easily,
now.

I watched my mother sink
deep into those dull waters,

and watch gasping friends
losing the threads of thought.

I am half aware
of lost connections,

realise the redundant questions
I begin to ask, misplaced.

I always remind myself
that Memory is the mother

of poetry,
and the spur

to jot things down
in recollection,

though sometimes I come
to this place wondering why.

Homebrew

The picking guitar
– electric, played finger style –

pushes through the speakers:
art, going back a generation,

caught by mechanics, electricity
riding me home to a time

of anticipation, the unknown,
my energies unguided.

Where was Mentor, then;
the art master; music school;

or Sybil, the cave-bound seer?
When time and space were roads

I was doubled up
in the demands of doubt.

Now I can tie up only
the home-forged things I learned

making mistakes, fretting
and picking with a purblind ear.

Spelling

Despite long and well-established use in S. Afr. Eng., neither the spelling nor the pronunciation of this word has become standardised.
– A Dictionary of South African English

The *leggevaan* stomps by
– this island reptile, blue-green
with a white spot low on his head,
like a third eye –

here called an *iguana*, or *l'iguana*,
which back home metamorphosed
through misunderstanding into *leguaan*,
or – on my child's tongue – *leggevaan*.

You need only see, in the sand cliff
of a lone river bank, a *leggevaan* hole
– the beast immersed in half-dark,
dead-still, half-in, half-out –

to leave in no doubt the hefty
amphibious influence of the word.

I recall *leggevaan*, conflate grammar,
draw the article into the noun,
change emphasis, recreate sense,
turn the rules of language upside down

– all these spellings run
in my mind as the creature
articulates by, her touching tongue,
split and slipping, tastes the ground.

I try to conjure the distant world
of her brain; hear the articulation
of her thoughts; invoke my reptile mind
and our kinship, rent by evolving time.

I watch her tail-tip drag off,
unseemly slow, and meekly towing
– the backward point that marks
the unaware, all our upside-down,

inside-out, arrogant
and back-to-front knowing.

Kestrel

Our windhover

It's easy now to slip uphill, in cars,
snaking up these smooth tarred roads
to the Valley of Desolation, sacrificing

all the slow and proper awe
a hiker earns, coming up the harder paths
through dolerite rock and mountain veld.

And down the beetling *kloofs* and *krantzes*,
we view the old and leafy frontier town
and her growing grey townships,

off-set and uncreative still, and sad
in that old South African way
that cleaves our landscapes, yet, and hearts.

But now a kestrel hovers
– just out there –
his wings stretched static

– fittingly a-flutter –
holding his position in the air,
lingeringly waiting, watchful,

hunting amongst the rock and scrub
for critters that scurry unaware

– as sharp-eyed time holds the skies,
watching us, with kestrel eyes.

Wells

I knelt because I was my mother,
I was the well of the world.
– Derek Walcott, 'Another Life'

i. The Seeping

Many a dwelling in this French village
has its old well still near the gate,
where to peer down into the earth
is to look back to the lost *lang syne*
and down past the moss-murk of rocks,
deep into the dark wet backwards of time.

Now, it is late autumn. The nut trees
loosely hold their last leaves,
the mist is settled, and all is deeply
quiet and presently contained.

Folk have burrowed out the insides
of these old homes, and made them warm
and modern, but the façades keep the past.
The thick moss on roof slates and on walls,
green and lush with growing,
holds a stillness that speaks with soft candour
of vanity, and far too gently of the rush
of human schemes, of all our slick knowing.

Everything seems so soundless, and nothing
appears to move in these autumn mists;
but slowly in subtle seeps of hours
the few leaves left on the cold, baring boughs

bend to their new brown; and, between
darknesses now, the hidden sun still slips.

ii. Memories

These wells in Africa suggest themselves:
out in sunlight, a colourful and loud
Nigerian courtyard, in sandy Kano,
the school well is bend-your-back low,
cemented square and sealed for safety
with a practical metal cover, locked secure.

There's no old tale in this new well,
but deep purposefulness. The drawing rope
is flat nylon webbing, black and rumpled
in the sun, its container is a rusty can
with a wire handle, lying idle: designed
unprettily, with a project pragmatism.

Yet it draws imagination, and draws
feelings back up, with telling old scenes
– the child, brought forward to recite
words from the Holy Koran; the robes
that bring to this place natural colour;
the old city's high walls of mud and sand
that speak of conflict, and community;

two desert men making their Hajj, tall
and robed, their wide eyes unfamiliar
with the airport, staring at my paler face,
at my bare head, my shirt, and western jeans
– big men, strong, rooted in the desert ways,
alien in the departure hall, holding hands.

iii. Aasvoëlkrans School

She's at the pump, the girl who cried
in class, who thought she couldn't
do the work, gasping with self-doubt,

the small, thin girl with little boots,
Sotho-speaking, her farm school
in these grasslands, far out from town:

she tugs the pump, for all she's worth,
the handle is higher than she – reaching,
and pulling down, laughing as she spouts

earth water for a classmate to catch,
her body pumping, gyring around,
drawing her balance from African earth.

iv. Well of Wells

Another is Sol Plaatje's well
in his old Boer War Mafeking
I was taken to, once, and given to drink:
a well he's said to have himself dug out.

And I quaffed the cool memories
of his ways, his belief in writing,
his faith that folk would read, and think,
and learn – so change would come;

how the word would bring wisdom
and from such knowledge, naturally
– and for him so clearly – would well
human kindness, to ease our long drought.

Weight

Struggle times, rural South Africa

A straggly funeral
along a hot dirt road outside Alice:
the mourners, poor village people,
decked as best they can, hot and tired,
the coffin weaving its weight,

so we stop, and lift our caps
to show the dead our respect:

when one breaks rank, steps
out of line to shout invective, spits
on the ground near his own feet.

I'm almost used to it,
this hatred of the times –

that old man who spits his long-held wrath
in my girlfriend's younger path,
she being as black as he,
her hand in mine an old betrayal;

the worker at the railway station
who spits in my face as he walks by

(but he is human and will look back,
so I wait, then raise a tired salute,

owning his anger, whence it comes;
and he does turn at last, raises
in kind his own surprised hand).

So now we pause
and face the mourner's ranting,
our caps still doffed
with a respect sad and heavy
in all that rage.

The Darkling Rainbow

Grahamstown, 1980s

The night she said yes – the dark
woman, my young heart's compass –
and loved me, overwhelming shyness
and the harsh sterility of our laws,
I left her rooms late, then walked
back into the deep apartheid night.

Like a vision – so sudden – the gloom
of campus was topped by a gush of light
and a small rainbow tinted the first mists
– and I in another world, seeing signs!

Till it struck me – a probing searchlight beam
cut across town, from the colonial
hillside fort to the township facing it.
The army, making free, played old wartime
searchlights down the dusty township roads,
asserting dread control and clear command,
taking any liberty – when uneasy time boiled
and rumbled against repression.

An anti-epiphany
– this spout of light mocked and soiled
everything, its small ironic rainbow
dancing still above the dark campus pines.

Philomel

Seized in flaps of fear
– his hawk-hands hold her fast –
she trembles, her dove
feathers red with the hurt.

Her brother-in-law keeps close
the tongue-cut girl, mutilated
in both mouth and cunt, fucking her
all through the sun-turning year.

Though in time, craftily she sews
her unflinching story, her art-voice
straight and true – untouched
by distancing mythology –

sewing her tapestry so clear
it makes her sister see all
and grasp the bewildered
innocence her story thrust

her into, unbidden:
her tongue torn out,
a twitching stump
in the all-silence,

broken by her straight
talking, softly woven stitch
by stitch, picking and unpicking
silent screaming art.

Poetry in South Africa

With the Helenvale Poets

We lock the gates
– security said we should –

with an iron chain
to keep the gangsters out,

though we know in fact
there's no keeping them at bay:

if they want to, they can come in,
into both your home and head

and do what it is they do.
But our poetry room is our retreat

where words are wrought,
so we lock the gate

to keep our comparisons safe,
our metaphors and meanings,

our alliteration and the rhyme,
the trickling stanzas, here

in this room, where we congregate
words, and sensitivity, and thought.

Feather Duster

In a post-colonial classroom

We teachers in the poorer schools
learn to use available resources
– and a feather duster is waiting there,
used and put aside, unnoticed almost
in its constant being, resting in its corner.
So we challenge the writers to see it,
to pick it up and dust with it, and write.

I've seen grey-black ostrich feathers fixed
to bamboo rods like these since childhood
and thought all the world an ostrich world,
with every pelmet swept, and spider corner
and dusty bookshelf, with large feathers
railed across the veld of the dry Karoo;

thought each town had a Feather Market Hall
where ostrich feathers were once bought
for fashionable London ladies' needs,
with crates weighed up and then shipped out;

supposed everybody knew of Oudtshoorn
where we saw ostriches up close and large,
bird-strange, and held in our young hands
our first heavy ostrich egg, the world's egg.

I see my mother, dusting. The kids write on,
lost in what they perceive. I must remember
not to do the tasks with them, lest I'm swept
away in whiffs of childhood dreams, and dust.

Serote

After thirty years' reading

In exile from Chile,
Allende said she most missed
the seasons of the year,

for Venezuela's equatorial green
was unchanging.

We are south enough
at home in Africa to feel
the blessed seasons,

the give-and-take
that patterns us,

the sun walking low up north
across the grey winter sky,
coming home for summer;

the Maluti snow, brown grass
or Highveld summer thunderstorms

sharing our political moods
as we know
that seasons come to pass.

Meditation Lesson

She led us to write down
all, all
our most beloved things,

each our own particular –
prompting jotting thoughts
as we worked our bits of paper.

When we were done –
winkling
from heart and fond recall

our most precious things,
reflecting,
self-satisfied –

she had us scrunch the page
and throw our notes away:
gone, at once

– to make a metaphor
of time's fell work
on everything we love.

There were words then
I wished I had not written,
to spook them with their names –

such is our spirited denial,
and holding off, that mad faith
in living that makes us us.

Today I reckon
that fleeting wasting time
is true to herself

as I watch
in the wind
the withering leaves.

The Move

We move today the non-profit office
from the street overlooking the bay
up the hill, to Upper Dickens Street,
to the old Catholic orphanage,

carrying, ferrying, dismantling
– all forms of deconstruction –
the guys lugging, strapping
desks and bookshelves to roof-racks,

loading the trailer, drinking warm water
– all day, till it's done: the old office
empty. The new is as semi-sorted
as a poem half-made, scrawled,

with revisions jotted across the page,
neither typed up, nor mulled over,
but an effort made, and a pledge
to the thought.

After the work, I walk
the grounds. Here, years ago,
our under-nine or -ten teams came
to play soccer against the orphan boys,
the urging Brothers on the side-lines

– but every game we'd beat the lads.
Now their soccer field is gone,
and retirement units ring the park.
The place has grown multi-purposefully.

But it keeps its own memory, like an elegy
not quite done, translating the older sounds
of young boys' tears and prayers, now mute,
into the older murmur of the frail-care wing.

Klein's *Trio*

Gideon Klein's work
cuts the auditorium air.

A few years ago
you and I trod the ghastly ground
out there, in Auschwitz,
feeling the shades' silences,

the big-eyed ghostliness
of camp and road-way,
of the barbed wire fence
in the Polish seasons.

In Auschwitz-Birkenau we saw
the track where the train chuffed in,
through the gate, to the terminal,
one coach still standing solo there.

I did not know, then,
hadn't heard Gideon Klein –
neither his life, nor music,
his heart, the bowing hopes
of his strings.

But here, where the viola
plucks his rhythm and the violin wails,
where the cello laments –

all comes into some brief
harmony, tripping
with that folk dance,

the train-like chugging rhythm
that calls us into the future
of our own past, dancing

and shunting with inevitable time
as death comes down
from the end of the line
hitching a partner of its own youth.

Rags of Time

It moves into high summer, far south
in Africa, with salt smells and breezes
off the seas. But in France, here,
a hemisphere away, it is late autumn.
Cold comes, and mists still the listless
lands. Fields lie long in their own being,
and crows speckle both earth and sky.

We will travel home soon, crossing seasons,
turning the paradoxes of distance
down into heat and wind and drought.

For now, this autumn, the garden nuts
fill our bowls. Cheeses and baguettes.
Wine from Bordeaux. Fire in the grate.

Rare friends during this year of deaths
have gone down into the backward dark;
but here is an old colleague in her home
in a French village, with a fire lit, books
and artworks, masks, husband, daughters.

We walk the woodland roads. A fence
at times keeps our way, or we baulk
at some beguiling path. Blackberries
and rosehips, perhaps a few mushrooms,
or hanging yellow leaves of the season
all tell how the earth rides the heavens
with our home-south closer to the sun,

whose distant light is weak here, and low.
I eye it with a weather eye. Our circle-slip
of time and that slight earth-tilt, I know,
are busy always: and make all the difference.

No Birds

The forest silence
is not dead. Dead is the pheasant
we find on the roadside,

still handsomely recognisable,
feathered,
but time-eaten from the inside.

The autumn forest is not dead.
And out in the farmlands
rooks, a jay, a robin
move silently. Crows
chase a pale hawk.

And back in the village,
a blackbird cries in the yard
of a house named *Le Chant des Oiseaux*.

This is a far countree.
The language is not my own.
I am a stranger. No birds sing
my tongue.

Feeling

In fallow lands rooks peck
and probe the soil and seagulls
with heads down keep foraging

as we tread the old village roads
and out between fields of kale, of beet
and some low uncertain autumn crops.

The friend's dogs we walk
pull at their leads, pull
with a leg-strength that doesn't let up

like the strange and strong, unseen
pull of the gravity that pulls
this memory down to write,

smelling new ways,
watching a great flock of birds
blur the horizon into a moving smudge:

we stand and watch, they're too far,
and we can guess, but never tell
what manner of birds they are.

No matter. We see: they play a part
in the impressionism of our lives
where truth is feeling and landscape,

unsure,
and pulling
art.

Cast

The immediate solidity
of the works, flesh bronze,
large hands,
strong thews and feet,

the from-every-angle cleverness
of the forms…

So,
in the garden of the museum
of Auguste Rodin,
quiet, not quite alone
but alone enough with these forms
of humanity, these solid shades,
these naked human allegories,
the damned, the suffering
and the serene;

the desperate burghers,

our divine and human comedies
play out

still, unmoving,

timeless

in this age of bronze.

Rodin

The leaves of the autumn trees
around Féricy were a sad rust-grey,
and those forest roads we walked
spilled into, influenced my mood
on our journey up to Paris to see
at last the life's work of Rodin
collected in this walled garden

where his figures, spaced about,
cast their own spell – these forms
shaped from his mind and feel,
the sensuous, moving, storied,
solid beings that tower over me.

In my mind, my own garden-stage,
I conjure you – for always I've wanted
to share flashes from encounters,
my brief allegories – but I see you only
as last I saw you, on your way to die,
walking awkwardly with a wheeled walker,
your heart and muscles wasting,
your loving, suffering body withering
like the forest leaves,
no strength left in your falling clay.

Love here is hefty and never-ending,
the large-limbed suffering is fixed,
the burghers still brood loss of town and being,
of citizenship and dignity, their bodies
tongues for pain:

I feel part of this drama
and yearn to speak to you
but language is stilled in my head,
forms fix, only the leaves of my mind
dry slowly, and darken. Allegories shape,
large and flesh and static.

In this garden enclosed,
I stand before The Gates of Hell.

At the Table in the *Pâtisserie*

I reflect on the garden
of art, Rodin's figures, green
and bronze in autumn light,
ham-fisted, big-bodied emotions,

humans, unclassically caught
in their moment, perfectly graceless
in dealing with things, their flesh
formed firm, as if time never twirls

– till a family comes in, a father
and his two small breathless girls,
to get their daily baguette
and the babbling sisters simply relish
pointing out and eyeing today's *éclairs* –

then out again the living go,
leaving me still with that garden
of passion affixed in my thought.

Scorpio

All great minds have bound themselves to some form of mechanical toil to obtain greater mastery of thought. Spinosa ground glasses for spectacles; Bayle counted the tiles on the roof; Montesquieu gardened.
– Balzac, 'Modeste Mignon'

The garden is marginal
and, like my thoughts, half-trained
and bewildered into some hope
of sweet disorder.

Yet there is peace in soil, a refuge,
a cleansing. The earth's loam stomach
is her bounty, too; her very give-and-take.
I mulch, and plant, harvest water, and feed.

The yield is small, but working soil
and plants is the learning of husbandry,
an echo of our human settlement,
the calendar work of time's turning year,
a restoration of the old crop goddesses,

from an age before those tradeful merchants
crossed the seas to gain rich earth-fruit
– plants, or minerals, or people, enslaved.
So I work the quiet mulch, move bricks,
bring hoe and rake and ready seed,

till there!
Stung by the scorpion.

A dozen cream-white scorplings
on her back, she scuttles and delves
quickly from sight. She is small,
but her poison sets my hand afire,
my spirit all aflutter.

She is dark, slight and slender of tail
and pincer and – as these words
attest – her sting is not fatal.

But while we treat the hand,
she slips the bucket with all her brood
back into the brown under-leaf
and melts again into the enclosed garden,

going to ground in my place of peace;
seeding for me
rich awareness of the older,

the unsettled
and earthy gods.

eDikeni

For Cheryl

Ntombiyamazangwa,
she said, the syllables and sounds
of a name bigger than herself
drawing me in, though I was already taken
by the small girl's strength of limb,
her wiry muscle activity,
her ready look-you-straight-in-the-face
frankness.

Her father walked to our home one night
with a vehicle stuck fifty miles away,
so he and I drove south, down
the Peddie road, to seek his son,
waiting with the stricken car.

Our headlights caught the genet,
broken-backed on the sand,
her front alive, her back legs dragging,
trying to tow herself clear:
this wiry catlike form, starkly dark-
and-white-patterned, fractured
and ghastly beautiful in the beam.

One direct blow with his tyre-lever
and the father stilled the struggle:
death can be as quick as life.
He laid the beast in the car boot,
keeping her for "traditional things"
– the genet has such markings,
such a tail…

Hours later we reached home
and I carried the limp-fleshed genet
up for you to see, her body sad,
utterly stark with her feline, foxy shape
and each careful mark of fur.

Then I passed her back
to Ntombiyamazangwa's careful father,
who took the beast and his sack of tools
across to their home, in the dark.

Crux

On my desk a Celtic cross
we bought in Dublin –

the human shape,
frail and exposed

against the circle's
eternity;

the human discomfort,
the learning,

the working through the real
to the real,

the unkind
feel of fact

touching
like a human finger bone

alive with flesh;
the need

to brace
for the self-horror

of truth:
the circle

against the frail
and relentlessly aware.

III

The dogstar's rabid. Our street
burns its spilt cabbage. Spent with heat
I brood on three good friends
dead in one year,
one summer's shock,
here where summer never ends.

– Derek Walcott, 'Dogstar'

Sitter

For Margaret Armoed

You've been alongside
the dead,

you tell me,
and have watched

them go,
reading their eyes.

People call me,
you rest your right hand

on your breast,
always to sit, so,

with their dying.
In their eyes

I see
what God will show.

Dié wat in die donker lê,
you add,

kom
tot die lig.

Nudge

After the McGregor Poetry Festival, 2017, and a poet dead

From solid words, hewn out,
I have come home to silence
and back to doubt; the diurnal
rounds haunted by thoughts
and odd images of old bones
scratched with symbolic script.

I'd call you out, but you are
but ashes now, God bless you,
stardust translated through
you to stardust, golden lad,
into new substantiality:

your old breath-words I find
written here should sprout
and nudge my barren mind,

but time twists and warps
everything upside down,
– stark and inside out.

Last Visit

Your being unresponsive,
you came into our house
like some Dadaist tortoise
following its own legs
– your walker,
and the Sphinx's riddle –

casting only frail eyes
upon us when we talked,
doing and getting done
and being done to, and
blessedly sleeping so
we could speak amongst
ourselves, of what was left
to say, at that broken time.

Once the house was quiet
and we two alone – we'd spent
mad times together, you and I,
reading, talking, drinking,
motorcycling, writing,
always working, courting
each our own way – alone I
said how good it was to see
you, host you in the home.
You said three words
only, the only three words
you said clear to me.
I am, you said, *kaput*.

You left, dragging remembrances
down the path with the walker.
There's no coming back, I thought.
And, of course, you died out west
past Knysna, a little way away,
somewhere between Cape Town
and here. And now.

Thought

In the pan, the smell
of my mother's mother frying
fish roe –

they found it, sometimes,
in the fish they bought,
the mother fish,

with swollen belly,
her eggs mellowing
when she was caught.

I never see fish roe now.
And grandma's dead
and gone.

I picked her up once,
when she fell
so much later on,

an old woman
and a cooking accident,
her wrists blistered,

and carried her to bed:
light as her sins
are now, her thought

and her dreams no more,
a thousand fish-spawn
dead.

Circumnavigation

For M.R. Marenene

We talk on the school steps
beneath the Zuurberg hills.
Memory,

I say, *that mother of all art*
and musing, is our keel,
ballast and sail, the chart

and compass of our long travail –
and now my own mother
lies listless in her doldrums,

as her memory drifts away.
Sensitive, you recall
your own mother's journey,

and explain the traditional take
on this human cycle:
how children, late arrivals

from their own world and words,
must be taught the tongue
of this our time, and their new place;

till, in the round of things, growing old,
they pull out ancient memories
to wear haphazard,

and pack our thoughts away,
and begin again to speak
with words and a tongue

we misunderstand
The words and thoughts
of their new clime,

bringing all things to one,
seem lost to reason,
confusing and distressing us

who struggle to grasp
the spellings
of a brave new time,

African Violet

Through all your dementia,
packing up always

to go home,
I marvel at the paradox,

the shifting stability,
that has become your time

and your sense of place.
And all through the packing

and repacking,
your African violet

shifts position,
from the counter to the box,

then into the safety
of your *Dieffenbachia* pot,

then up on a table,
and down and out on the floor:

but the violet flowers
have never wavered or blinked,
and keep smiling out their smiling sex,
whether their pot would dip today, or rise,

and they'll keep me stable
until the last blossom dies.

At Work

Afternoon heat. The old flat
on the beachfront, Summerstrand.
The swirl of wind. A truck runs
its throbbing diesel engine.
In her old Prefect car with a radiator
that leaks warm drops of rusty water,
the car seats hot in their own smell,
long after lunch, my mother brought
us all to the beach: we'll go home soon.

My mother laughs with an aunt –
both have since grown old, and died,
their voices drift on the breeze.

This morning she lugs the washing across
the lawn to the lines that my father strung.
Near the wall is the garden he made,
setting old concrete slabs for the beds.
The parsley grows hidden, dark and low;
the celery stands lighter green, and tall.
When I am sent to cut some for the pot
or salad, I never remember which is which,
and my mother explains time and again.
My father is at work. Through long hours
he's at work, well into the stretch of time,
and we, for all time, waiting.

As my mother's widow memory goes,
she endlessly asks, *where is your father*?
But she resigns herself, knows:

He's at work still. I have spent
my whole life waiting for him.

And so we wait, as the doves call
away the long afternoon.

Mater Dei

There's nowhere left
for this old somebody to rest
or wander, this cold dusk,
holding out his bowl
for scraps of kindness,

hungering for a word
to hint that all is not lost;
that his threadbare flesh
a heavy woman once washed
in tender days is not all fault;

that his torn
and timeworn being
– sniffing still for whiffs
of her old and festive oven –
is not all done:

this dusk, his old mind fathoms
that missing mother-care could
figure all love, and may perhaps
suggest all spirit, boundless,
elusive and free,

while he holds in trust
– soliciting unsound scraps
of second-hand words –
his empty bowl of wood.

Earthy

On the muddy mangrove banks,
hand-large crabs
slip sidewards into holes

like ghosts withdrawing
from the coming light.

Nearer the water, the crabs
are small, one arm overgrown
and pale

and they hold the big claw
out to him warningly
as they scuttle sidelong,
clearing footfall space.

This is their place.
He intrudes on their otherness
as the dawn does on darkness,

he feels them all around,
like wraiths withdrawing,
watching stalk-eyed,

creeping into sideway tunnels.

Silent crabs,
like conscience in dreams
waking with the light,

living stalk-eyed,
making inside images of him
in the very mud of things.

Mangrove Mud

Leisurely, the egret
on the mud tablet stamps its hieroglyph.
– Derek Walcott, *'Another Life'*

All is still:
the bare trees, bone-grey,
reflect on listless waters

like unforgetfulness,
like death-twists in wood.

Only some little egrets –
white, white, and there, white

living specks – pick quietly
along the slow mud shadows

or perch unmoving
on the stark branches.

All is fixed, as set as art
where the osprey perches
in her as-she-did-before place,
her wings settled, dark;

the scene like a canvas
– some grotesque still life –
with dead-grey branches
that ghost the afternoon light,

tangled, twisted in an agony
of old dying. All is lifeless now,
in this disremembered space,
this word-image scene
of no forgetting.

The Bay

For Hilary Graham

Here's Graham's *The Artist Turns his Back*
on the Bay. For years I've known this canvas
but never so wet-oil fresh in my eyes
as now, up from the South End Museum,
from histories of the quick heart-crossed pain
of a port-people so smashed in their kin,
their houses razed, and kith driven away,
leaving this veld wasted with lost cries
and wretched anger.

Here, the artist spurns the wrack
of the old sea-front homes.
But mostly he leaves the shameless realm
of the self-righteous, the demolishers,

the watchers who lick themselves. He scorns
the bay where their forebears beached.

The apartheid flag still waves:
life flutters on, like the torturer's idle horse,
or Brueghel's lone ploughman tilling.
There's the tugboat busy, busy steaming
out on the pain-dark sea…

Through these ruins of place and soul
the artist strides, defiant and back-turned,
carrying his own passion and visions,
hefting a pair of completed canvasses.

Over his shoulder
he bears brushes of new sights, new notions,
while he steps out strong, like a matador.
The people jeer and roar, and sneer farewells.
One character bares an awesome bum.

He strides past the women,
leaving sins in the ruined land,
the wasteland wilderness of this city –
this rough bay that I've come back to, wasted
in myself, to plant these prodigal words.

Sein

My skin eats
terribly at me,
finding such a softness of psyche,

like a crab
nibbling
into mind;

I find my being
in our post-colony: this salty time,
this muddy bank

– I hear the quick,
warm hands of Rilke's words
make a gesture of *to be*

briefly, before
the voice is broken
again –

alive
to the quick history
that becomes our skin.

Grackles

I set the breakfast down,
but need to go to fetch the water
– it's tropical hot here,
in this island torrid zone –

and I come back to birds
– grackles, black and brown,
at the plate – dipping beaks deep
into all my scrambled egg.

Hey! I tell them off,
and away they flit
like dawn-lit dreams.
But my egg is eaten into.

I wonder about bacteria,
micro-organisms, about bird flu.
Separating a bit off,
I say, *You'll get that later,*

then tuck into the rest.
Ag, I could share it with them
properly, but humans are all around
making me stiff and stern.

But the birds eye me,
seeing me, knowing better –
waiting on the fence.

Art on Art

An old man, a few rows forward,
sketches the violinist. She bows
with vigour and with luxury, quicker
than the careful violist, or the cellist.

She has more leg placed
out from her red dress,
and plays and leans and cuts
into the air figures half formed

till the Baroque of Purcell
floats statuesque, in such sound
and mutual art that thought floats
and fiddles in the formal night

and settles on the artist's page;
while the cellist, in blue,
bows her bass, adept in the undertows
and water-weedy sonorous,

till these draperies of sound
enfold the man who draws
the violinist – and me, noting his
drawing, and writing him down.

Shell

Hermit crabs walk the land,
here, bearing borrowed shells.

Along the mud pathway
a shell stops and wobbles
– the crab legs are drawn in
until the shell lies dead.

Here, a crab in a shell
tries to make me believe
this homely shell is but
a random thing, dead in itself,

using her house of metaphor
so well in her poetry
of the pathway,

keeping herself safe
in a dead shell
alive
with suggestion.

Wasps

...grace doesn't destroy nature but perfects it...
– Thomas Aquinas, *Summa Theologica*

Nature perfected might seem
to be the very breath of bliss,

though when I think of nature
I recall two wasps I saw hunting,
fixed on a flying moth, following
with computer-locked efficiency;

or that yellow-legged wasp clutching
a spider's body, the spider legs
bitten off and eight stumps stirring
the pointless air:

the wasp keeps the stung
prey for fresh living food
her larva will hatch
from an egg, carefully laid
upon the afflicted spider
so that her young can suckle
on the unescaping flesh alive.

Nature can be stark,
and wasp mother-care chilling

– till nature perfected becomes
as much mystery to me as grace.

Metaphors

The crabs here: I like them.
The little fiddler crabs
with one large claw
as bold as a violin thrust out

– and when he feeds with the other,
Voilà! It's a fiddler bowing;
or the hermit crabs
dragging borrowed shells

out onto the mud. At home,
our hermits seem more careful,
keeping to the pools and rocks –
but these hermits are pilgrims.

I like their metaphors, and I smile,
aware that it is all in my head,
and if I were dead they'd nibble
away at my flesh, like a cancer.

Critic

The day squalls and spits rain
and the island is grey,
coconut palms bend and bow
to the winds.

He makes tea and writes,
trying to find what he thinks,
to articulate wind-blown words
together.

This morning was fine,
and he holds the swamp in mind,
where the heron kicked up the mud,
her neck waiting with beaky eye,

the stern critic,
minding carelessness,
her neck muscle-taut
with curled back, a tight-sprung
ready hunger.

The heron knows
it's the chaos of things
that'll flush out the hidden.

Metamorphosis

Old chaos first crystallised into law,
Ovid says, and then slowly melted down
till we have today, where the wild weather
roams and the oceans come, all Poseidon
in their shoulders, rising.

We ourselves can see the water
finding out foundations, seaweed
growing in the certainty, limpets
across your conscience, pearls
that were your eyes.

I recall a print framed in a pub:
Georgian gentry weigh trout,
noting their catches in their book,
weighing and recording, the records
finding out the laws of nature.
Through the casement, the Anglican church
tower is square and solid stone.

But how the south winds of change
have blown, and the hard rain
rains down every day

till we see that those men
weighed not fish,
but the weight of their own beings,
their own fat consciences,

heavier than the truth
in a simple ostrich feather.

Tree Fuchsia

I neglect most shamefully
my bonsais, which grow unkempt –
the original sin against living art.

I told her once, my psychologist friend,
when she would fathom the state of my soul
she should simply read my house plants –

for psyche will flourish with them
when I finger time, and snip and tend,
otherwise all grows dry, and spent.

Then she asked, of all trees, which I
loved most. I never own favourites,
but said, at that time, the tree fuchsia:

while not a limber bonsai tree, indeed,
in untouched veld she will bloom little spurts
of orange-red, deep on her inner stems.

She, the psychologist always, granted
– giving no reason then, or why –
that my choice rang true to her, for me.

But, I confess, I am so self-sinful
that I neglect – fighting the sea
of time and the old world's business –

the trees of my life, my dear bonsais.

Thread

In memoriam: Viv England, Mike Snyman, Norman Morrissey

It's the frailty
– the thin thread of life.

I've breathed words
from tentative scripts
at memorials for three friends
this year, alone:

and my heart is as dull
as our hollow
water-tank, bass-toned
this drought.

I miss each one, dearly,
their dreams now done.

I watched their paths fade
into sick-beds,
death beds,
heard the death rattle, thrice.

I see what we are: our way
strips back, and narrows.

And yet this morning,
my dead bougainvillea bonsai,
a cascade I'd given up on,

there: tiny shoots on her tips.

Stella Maris, Semper Virgo

Le Gosier, Guadeloupe

Walking randomly in town,
as I like to do, enabling
the unexpected, I find myself
strolling up a road that rolls

down past the empty stadium,
past the lonely lagoon
of the multitudinous crab-folk,
the wet bird-print mud and smells,

and out to sea; my mind wandering
always to the slave narratives
I read by night; fathoming other
walkers and their long shadows.

I feel myself trailing clouds
of history, where everything I am
has become accusation – my language,
being and education, work: and all.

A small child is walking up – blue top,
white shorts and skinny dark legs,
her hair that homely African swathe –
it's her world. Giving her space

I look down, hear a tiny *Bonjour.*
An old man's heart is easily rent;
as meek words drop and bless,
I am part of a world, a brief humanity,

and I am grasping for French.
Bonjour, I respond, late, forlorn
– a forgetful elder, wondering
how caught I am by virgin kindness.

La Grande Soufrière

From the mangrove swamp
with its rich and static waters,
dark and brown-black blue,
the path snakes through the margin zone
of those worldly yellow hibiscus trees
and quickly out to the clear lap of ocean.

Beyond – across the broad bay sweep –
is the opaque blue mountain
of the bigger island. Volcanic,
silent and softly grand, the great
sulphur gate, hunching its strength,
and waiting…

But here, just in from the sea
– just a lazy stone-toss length –
is a small building, dirty white
and cracked, seeming to be
an unkempt restroom, crouched
with that windowless threat:
and I skirt it, circumspect,

turn to find it is a simple shrine,
light blue walls inside, a ceiling black
with holy candle soot; floor and shelf busy
with icons, crucifixes and fresh flowers.

In this world of such wear and tear,
I find myself in a glade with flitting
hummingbirds and bird song,

where, just steps from our uncertain sea,
a small shrine has candles burning
for Mary, *Notre Dame de la Mer*.

Latterday

I have come full circle;
once an old, old child
– God's trustworthy –

now a puerile elder
in the making
– as trustworthy as hell –

seeping wit like a sieve,
worn and rusted, wetting
like an infant, like a well,

and leaks will run to nothing.
I'll roll my trouser legs
and wade to new paddocks,

and let anyone ask why,
I know, I can tell:
I have come full circle, I.

Permissions and Acknowledgements

Versions of some of these poems ('African Violet', 'Circumnavigation', 'The Weight', 'Kestrel', 'Tree Fuchsia', 'Deads' Town Path' and 'Serote') have appeared in the annual collections of the Ecca group, Hogsback, and others ('Spelling' and 'eDikeni') in *New Contrast*. A version of 'The Darkling Rainbow' has appeared in *Coming Home: Poems of the Grahamstown Diaspora* edited by Harry Owen (East London: Poets Printery, 2019). An early version of 'The Bay' appeared in *Beneath the Bridge of Metaphors: Poems from NMMU Arts and Culture Workshops* edited by Brian Walter (Nelson Mandela University, Arts and Culture, 2014).

Permissions to cite Derek Walcott and Amos Tutuola in epigraphs have been gratefully obtained from Faber and Faber, and from Oxford University Press for the extract from *A Dictionary of South African English on Historical Principles*.

Phrases, epigraphs and quotations have been used, sometimes with and sometimes without acknowledgement from the following sources:

Page v
Still at work, time shifts the stanzas,
scratches a line, evokes – for unity –
an old theme again, always moving chunks
of life away from childhood, and into age.
Brian Walter

Page 1
He told us that both white and black deads were living in the Deads' Town, not a single alive was there at all. Because everything that they were doing there was incorrect to alives and everything that all alives were doing was incorrect to deads too.
Amos Tutuola, *The Palm-Wine Drinkard* (London: Faber and Faber, 1985)

Page 2
I did not satisfy with it as palm-wine.
Amos Tutuola, *The Palm-Wine Drinkard* (London: Faber and Faber, 1985)

Page 5
… the gentleman left the really road
on which we were travelling and branched
into an endless forest…
Amos Tutuola, *The Palm-Wine Drinkard* (London: Faber and Faber, 1985)

Page 11

Past thirty now I know
To love the self is dread
Of being swallowed by the blue
Of heaven overhead
Or rougher blue below.
Derek Walcott, 'Crusoe's Island' in *The Poetry of Derek Walcott 1948–2013* selected by Glyn Maxwell (New York: Farrar, Straus and Giroux, 2014)

Page 19

Now, at the rising of Venus – the steady star
that survives translation, if one can call this lamp
the planet that pierces us over indigo islands –
despite the critical sand flies, I accept my function
as a colonial upstart at the end of an empire,
a single, circling, homeless satellite.
Derek Walcott, 'North and South' in *The Poetry of Derek Walcott 1948–2013* selected by Glyn Maxwell (New York: Farrar, Straus and Giroux, 2014)

Page 22

Despite long and well-established use in S. Afr. Eng., neither the spelling nor the pronunciation of this word has become standardised.
A Dictionary of South African English on Historical Principles (Oxford: Oxford University Press, 1996)

Page 25

I knelt because I was my mother,
I was the well of the world.
Derek Walcott, 'Another Life' in *The Poetry of Derek Walcott 1948–2013* selected by Glyn Maxwell (New York: Farrar, Straus and Giroux, 2014)

Page 49

All great minds have bound themselves to some form of mechanical toil to obtain greater mastery of thought. Spinosa ground glasses for spectacles; Bayle counted the tiles on the roof; Montesquieu gardened.
Honoré de Balzac, 'Modeste Mignon' in *Collected Works of Honoré de Balzac (1799–1850)* (Hastings: Delphi Classics, 2014)

Page 55

The dogstar's rabid. Our street
burns its spilt cabbage. Spent with heat
I brood on three good friends
dead in one year,
one summer's shock,
here where summer never ends.

Derek Walcott, 'Dogstar' in Derek Walcott *Poems 1965–1980* (London: Jonathan Cape, 1992)

Page 69

Leisurely, the egret
on the mud tablet stamps its hieroglyph.
Derek Walcott, 'Another Life' in *The Poetry of Derek Walcott 1948–2013* selected by Glyn Maxwell (New York: Farrar, Straus and Giroux, 2014)

Page 71

Hilary Graham's *The Artist Turns his Back on the Bay*, 1998, oil on board, Nelson Mandela Metropolitan Art Museum. The image has been reproduced with the kind permission of the Nelson Mandela Metropolitan Art Museum and Hilary Graham.

Page 77

. . . grace doesn't destroy nature but perfects it…
Thomas Aquinas, *Summa Theologica: From the Complete American Edition* translated by the Fathers of the Dominican Province (Kindle edition, Coyote Canyon Press)

OTHER WORKS IN THE DRYAD PRESS LIVING POETS SERIES

AVAILABLE NOW

Otherwise Occupied, Sally Ann Murray
Landscapes of Light and Loss, Stephen Symons
An Unobtrusive Vice, Tony Ullyatt
A Private Audience, Beverly Rycroft
Metaphysical Balm, Michèle Betty

FORTHCOMING IN 2019

happier were the victims, Kambani Ramano

OTHER WORKS BY DRYAD PRESS (PTY) LTD

Unearthed: A Selection of the Best Poems of 2016,
edited by Joan Hambidge and Michèle Betty
The Coroner's Wife: Poems in Translation, Joan Hambidge

Available in South Africa from better bookstores, internationally from African Books Collective (www.africanbookscollective.com) and online at www.dryadpress.co.za

Printed in the United States
By Bookmasters